Partnerships for Emerging Research Institutions

REPORT OF A WORKSHOP

I0896216

Committee on Partnerships for Emerging Research Institutions

Policy and Global Affairs

NATIONAL ACADEMY OF ENGINEERING *AND*
NATIONAL RESEARCH COUNCIL
OF THE NATIONAL ACADEMIES

THE NATIONAL ACADEMIES PRESS
Washington, D.C.
www.nap.edu

THE NATIONAL ACADEMIES PRESS 500 Fifth Street, N.W. Washington, DC 20001

NOTICE: The project that is the subject of this report was approved by the Governing Board of the National Research Council, whose members are drawn from the councils of the National Academy of Sciences, the National Academy of Engineering, and the Institute of Medicine. The members of the committee responsible for the report were chosen for their special competences and with regard for appropriate balance.

This study was supported by the National Academy of Sciences. Any opinions, findings, conclusions, or recommendations expressed in this publication are those of the author(s) and do not necessarily reflect the views of the organizations or agencies that provided support for the project.

International Standard Book Number-13: 978-0-309-13083-7
International Standard Book Number-10: 0-309-13083-2

Additional copies of this report are available from the National Academies Press, 500 Fifth Street, N.W., Lockbox 285, Washington, DC 20055; (800) 624-6242 or (202) 334-3313 (in the Washington metropolitan area); Internet, *http://www.nap.edu*.

Copyright 2009 by the National Academy of Sciences. All rights reserved.

Printed in the United States of America

THE NATIONAL ACADEMIES

Advisers to the Nation on Science, Engineering, and Medicine

The **National Academy of Sciences** is a private, nonprofit, self-perpetuating society of distinguished scholars engaged in scientific and engineering research, dedicated to the furtherance of science and technology and to their use for the general welfare. Upon the authority of the charter granted to it by the Congress in 1863, the Academy has a mandate that requires it to advise the federal government on scientific and technical matters. Dr. Ralph J. Cicerone is president of the National Academy of Sciences.

The **National Academy of Engineering** was established in 1964, under the charter of the National Academy of Sciences, as a parallel organization of outstanding engineers. It is autonomous in its administration and in the selection of its members, sharing with the National Academy of Sciences the responsibility for advising the federal government. The National Academy of Engineering also sponsors engineering programs aimed at meeting national needs, encourages education and research, and recognizes the superior achievements of engineers. Dr. Charles M. Vest is president of the National Academy of Engineering.

The **Institute of Medicine** was established in 1970 by the National Academy of Sciences to secure the services of eminent members of appropriate professions in the examination of policy matters pertaining to the health of the public. The Institute acts under the responsibility given to the National Academy of Sciences by its congressional charter to be an adviser to the federal government and, upon its own initiative, to identify issues of medical care, research, and education. Dr. Harvey V. Fineberg is president of the Institute of Medicine.

The **National Research Council** was organized by the National Academy of Sciences in 1916 to associate the broad community of science and technology with the Academy's purposes of furthering knowledge and advising the federal government. Functioning in accordance with general policies determined by the Academy, the Council has become the principal operating agency of both the National Academy of Sciences and the National Academy of Engineering in providing services to the government, the public, and the scientific and engineering communities. The Council is administered jointly by both Academies and the Institute of Medicine. Dr. Ralph J. Cicerone and Dr. Charles M. Vest are chair and vice chair, respectively, of the National Research Council.

www.national-academies.org

COMMITTEE ON PARTNERSHIPS FOR EMERGING RESEARCH INSTITUTIONS

JULIET GARCIA (*Chair*), President, University of Texas at Brownsville
ERROLL B. DAVIS, JR., Chancellor, University System of Georgia
DARYUSH ILA, Director, Alabama A&M Research Institute
WAYNE P. JOHNSON, Vice President for University Relations, Hewlett-Packard Company
VIJAYA MELNICK, Director of the Office of Sponsored Programs, University of the District of Columbia
TERRENCE S. MILLAR, Professor of Mathematics, University of Wisconsin-Madison
DIANA S. NATALICIO, President, University of Texas at El Paso
T. JOAN ROBINSON, Provost and Vice President for Academic Affairs, Morgan State University
JUAN M. SANCHEZ, Vice President for Research, University of Texas at Austin
MARCUS W. SHUTE, Vice President for Research and Sponsored Programs, Tennessee State University

Project Staff

EARNESTINE PSALMONDS,* Visiting Scholar, National Science Foundation
MERRILEA MAYO, Director, Government-University-Industry Research Roundtable (until November 2007)
CATHERINE DIDION, Senior Program Officer, National Academy of Engineering
DENISE GREENE, Administrative Coordinator, Government-University-Industry Research Roundtable

*Earnestine Psalmonds is a visiting scholar from the National Science Foundation (NSF) at the National Research Council. This work was supported by NSF, but findings, conclusions, or recommendations expressed are those of the authoring committee and do not necessarily reflect the views of NSF.

Preface

Strengthening the science and engineering enterprise is key to positioning the United States so that it can remain globally competitive well into the future. As recognized in the National Academies report, *Rising Above the Gathering Storm*,[1] much of our success as a nation relies on our investments in basic research and on our ability to educate the populace, and educate them well. While higher education is increasingly seen as a private good—the means to personal economic advancement—it continues to also be an important public good, critical for the advancement of the nation.

The United States has achieved world prominence in higher education primarily through a unique blend of research and teaching at universities. Most studies on the impact of research in higher education focus on research universities.[2] However, according to Fall 2005 enrollment data, about 75 percent of all U.S. undergraduate students are currently enrolled at other types of institutions.[3] Further, these other

[1]NAS, NAE, and IOM. 2007. Rising Above the Gathering Storm: Energizing and Employing America for a Brighter Economic Future. Washington, DC: The National Academies Press.

[2]For purposes of this report, these are defined as research universities (very high and high research activity) and doctoral/research universities according to the 2005 Carnegie Classification.

[3]National Science Foundation, Division of Science Resources Statistics, Special Tabulations of U.S. Department of Education, National Center for Education Statistics, Integrated Postsecondary Education Data System, Fall Enrollment Survey, 2005.

institutions encompass the bulk of the minority student population in the United States—a population that is large and growing. What happens in these institutions matters, and will matter, quite profoundly for our collective future.

Providing more opportunities for student participation in research in these institutions can help strengthen our scientific sector. Research experience is now known to be an extremely effective means for engaging students, especially in science and engineering, yet it is not used extensively to engage a large segment of the student population. The reasons for this phenomenon were examined in a September 13, 2007, National Academies workshop entitled "Partnerships for Emerging Research Institutions" (ERIs). This report summarizes those discussions.

Workshop participants included research administrators, deans and provosts, department chairs, faculty researchers, presidents of institutions and university systems, and representatives from federal agencies and laboratories. The participants acknowledged that there are differences between public and private institutions, and that the issues raised in the report would vary accordingly.

The workshop began by examining the impact of research experiences on students in ERIs. It then dissected the reasons why it is so difficult to cultivate a research climate in these institutions. Workshop participants discussed three interrelated problems. First, teaching loads at ERIs are usually double or triple that of research universities. There is simply no time to do research. Second, many ERIs are extremely limited in the amount of centralized support they can offer their research-performing faculty. From the faculty viewpoint, this makes conducting research in the limited time available substantially more challenging and time-consuming. When resources such as sponsored research personnel, intellectual property offices, and business support services are minimal, the associated administrative duties fall squarely on the researchers themselves. These dual problems of limited time, and spending that time to perform multiple, extra administrative functions can be overwhelming. Third, the faculty reward system does not compensate adequately for the daunting burdens that ERI researchers must bear, or for the full scope of their efforts. The net result is that few ERI faculty pursue research, leaving most of our nation's students without access to the one experience that is the foundation of the science and engineering disciplines.

The workshop did present hope, however. In these pages the reader will find some creative solutions presented by workshop participants to both the teaching load and "administructural" problems that plague administrators and faculty dedicated to actively engaging their institutions in research. Many of these solutions involve partnerships with other institutions or organizations; hence, the word "partnerships" in the title of the workshop. We hope that this report is useful, but more important, we encourage a serious re-examination of how to retool our institutions and the nation to provide one of the most powerful educational interventions to a large segment of the population.

Juliet Garcia, *Chair*
Committee on Partnerships for
Emerging Research Institutions

Acknowledgments

This report has been reviewed in draft form by individuals chosen for their diverse perspectives and technical expertise, in accordance with procedures approved by the National Academies' Report Review Committee. The purpose of this independent review is to provide candid and critical comments that will assist the institution in making its published report as sound as possible and to ensure that the report meets institutional standards for quality and objectivity. The review comments and draft manuscript remain confidential to protect the integrity of the process.

We wish to thank the following individuals for their review of this report: Tabbetha Dobbins, Louisiana Tech University; Cathy Fore, Oak Ridge Associated Universities; Francisco Gonzalez-Lima, University of Texas-Austin; Harold Hellenbrand, California State University, Northridge; Mildred Ofosu, Morgan State University; Beheruz Sethna, University of West Georgia; and Gerald Van Hecke, Harvey Mudd College.

Although the reviewers listed above have provided many constructive comments and suggestions, they were not asked to endorse the content of the report, nor did they see the final draft before its release. Responsibility for the final content of this report rests entirely with the authoring committee and the institution.

Contents

TABLES

FIGURES

BOXES

Introduction

Colleges and universities engage in research and development—*faculty-directed non-sponsored research* to understand existing knowledge through the process of inquiry and exploration; *basic research* to expand knowledge or understanding of phenomena without a goal of specific applications toward processes or products; *applied research* to determine possible uses for the results of basic research, thereby discovering new scientific knowledge with specific commercialization objectives; and *development* to use the knowledge gained from research to produce useful materials, devices, systems, or methods, including the design and development of prototypes and processes.[1]

With no nationally supported system of higher education, the United States spends little on faculty-directed and undergraduate research. There is significant funding for basic and applied research, primarily through the federal science agencies—the National Institutes of Health (NIH), the National Science Foundation (NSF), the National Aeronautics and Space Administration (NASA), portions of the Department of Defense (DOD), portions of the Department of Energy (DOE), and more. With respect to development activities, these also are nationally funded, through DOD 6.3 Advanced Development and 6.4 Demonstration/Validation funding available to industry, for programs such as the Small Business Innovation Research (SBIR) program, or through the federal laboratories housed within various agencies.

[1]National Science Foundation. 2008. Science and Engineering Indicators.

Basic research is largely concentrated in this nation's research universities. However, as recent reports imply, there is a need to broaden the base of universities that can undertake such research so that the United States can remain a leader in the global economy (Hauger and McEnaney, 2000). Most colleges and universities are not classified as research universities and conduct little ongoing sponsored basic research. Originally, the intent of the September 2007 workshop, "Partnerships for Emerging Research Institutions" (ERIs), was to examine access to research at institutions receiving less than $15 million a year in federally sponsored research.[2] As the committee planned the workshop, however, it became evident that the issues and solutions were far more generic and applied to all but the research universities. For the purposes of this report, therefore, ERIs include all master's colleges and universities, baccalaureate colleges, and tribal colleges according to the 2005 Carnegie Classification system (see Appendix D).

The questions addressed in the workshop were:

1. What does the presence or absence of basic research signify for student achievement?
2. What obstacles currently preclude access to research for ERIs?
3. What approaches can be used to overcome these obstacles?

The workshop did *not* focus on the lack of research equipment or research funding as obstacles. The inability to compete for resources instead was regarded as a symptom of more fundamental structural deficiencies. Two categories of barriers were discussed in depth at the workshop: (1) a severe lack of time for teaching-intensive faculty to conduct research, and (2) insufficient administrative infrastructure to support even the modest daily routines required by a research enterprise.

THE IMPORTANCE OF EMERGING RESEARCH INSTITUTIONS

Emerging Research Institutions (master's colleges and universities, baccalaureate colleges, and tribal colleges) constitute one-third (1,463) of the 4,392 institutions of higher education that are listed in the 2005 Carnegie Classification system (see Appendix D), and they enroll over 30 percent of the U.S. post-secondary student population (see Figure 1). In

[2]The Federal Demonstration Partnership (FDP) defines Emerging Research Institutions as institutions whose federal obligations are less than $20 million annually for research and development and are funded by at least two FDP federal agencies. Institutions whose annual federally supported expenditures are less than $15 million may participate in FDP activities.

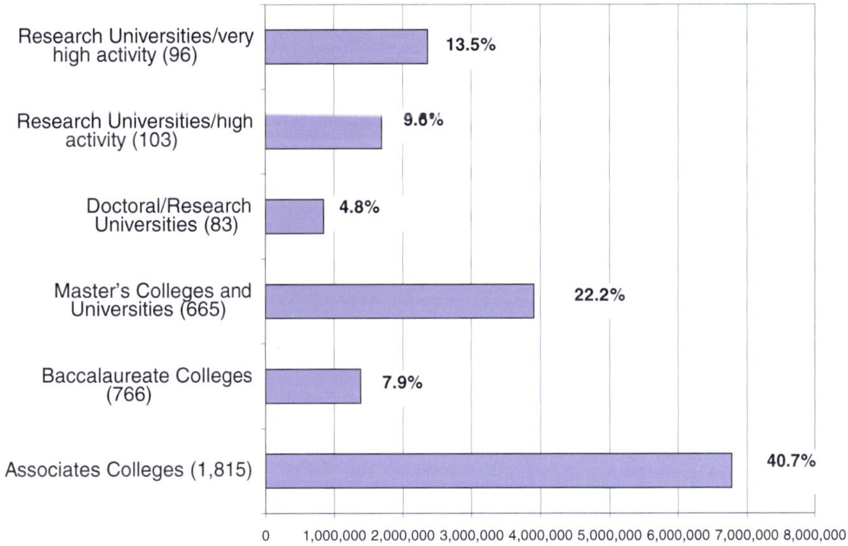

FIGURE 1 Basic Carnegie classification: distribution of institutions and percentage of total enrollment, 2005.
NOTE: Fall enrollment may not reflect the total number of students served over the course of a year. Tribal colleges (32) account for 0.10% of total enrollment.
SOURCE: 2005 Carnegie Classification; National Center for Education Statistics, IPEDS Fall Enrollment (2004).

addition, excluding the associate colleges, they enroll the largest number of undergraduates and the largest proportion of the minority student population, as shown in Table 1 and Figure 2.

Many workshop participants shared the belief that ERIs potentially can contribute more significantly to innovative research and *must* play a more prominent role in sustaining the nation's technological competitiveness. However, the research universities receive 83 percent of total federal obligations for research and development (R&D), according to NSF FY 2005 data (Table 2). Moreover, federal academic science and engineering (S&E) obligations totaled $28.3 billion in FY 2005, and the leading 20 universities (ranked in terms of total S&E obligations) received 34 percent of that total. Generally, ERIs also reflect a relatively low level of research activity as measured by science and engineering (S&E) R&D expenditures, non-S&E R&D expenditures, and S&E research staff (postdoctoral appointees and non-faculty research staff with doctorates).[3]

[3]The Carnegie Foundation for the Advancement of Teaching, March 7, 2006.

TABLE 1 Enrollment in All Fields, by Race/Ethnicity and 2005 Carnegie Classification of Schools, Fall 2005

Enrollment and Race/Ethnicity	Total	Emerging Research Universities	Research Institutions	Associate's Colleges	Special Focus
Undergraduate enrollment	14,514,807	3,508,655	4,415,845	6,326,050	264,257
American Indian or Alaska Native	142,169	27,153	38,097	65,273	11,646
Asian or Pacific Islander	883,526	281,754	184,630	405,563	11,579
Black, Non-Hispanic	1,730,322	324,002	564,087	815,855	26,378
Hispanic	1,705,019	272,690	460,436	943,085	28,808
White, Non-Hispanic	8,892,473	2,302,934	2,789,892	3,654,485	145,162
Other/Unknown Race & Ethnicity	855,930	197,187	278,372	347,931	32,440
Temporary Resident	305,368	102,935	100,331	93,858	8,244
Graduate enrollment	2,160,672	1,229,305	821,191	628	109,548
American Indian or Alaska Native	11,735	6,381	4,708	0	646
Asian or Pacific Islander	100,101	62,361	30,514	4	7,222
Black, Non-Hispanic	198,023	92,767	95,909	67	9,280
Hispanic	136,890	62,471	65,435	6	8,978
White Non-Hispanic	1,239,246	681,210	494,774	532	62,730
Other/Unknown Race & Ethnicity	215,845	114,765	90,992	17	10,071
Temporary Resident	258,832	209,350	38,859	2	10,621

NOTE: Special focus institutions also include tribal colleges and institutions not classified.
SOURCE: National Science Foundation, Division of Science Resources Statistics, special tabulations of U.S. Department of Education. National Center for Education Statistics, Integrated Postsecondary Education Data System, Fall Enrolment Survey, 2005.

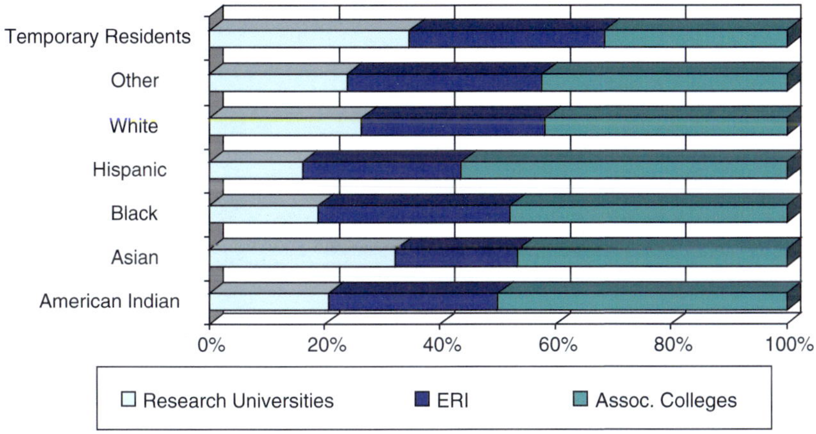

FIGURE 2 Percent undergraduate enrollment by race/ethnicity and Carnegie classification, Fall 2005.
SOURCE: National Science Foundation, Division of Science Resources Statistics, special tabulations of U.S. Department of Education. National Center for Education Statistics, Integrated Postsecondary Education Data System, Fall Enrollment Survey, 2005.

Some ERIs are in a unique position to provide access and opportunity to underserved populations, including minorities and the economically disadvantaged. For example, Benjamin Flores described the University of Texas at El Paso's mandate to serve the region: to provide the resources and the education necessary for the region to thrive economically. He reiterated the importance of research in stating that it enables the institution to create, interpret, validate, and apply disseminated knowledge. He added, "But we also want to attract and retain a diverse and innovative faculty that will be dedicated to both teaching and research." This is a compelling statement about the impact of ERIs in producing the next generation of science, technology, engineering, and math (STEM) knowledge workers.

Workshop participants attested to their research capabilities that are largely untapped and provided testimonials about their graduates who have proven to be highly competitive for graduate school and the job market. In addition, they stressed the fact that, when given the opportunity to compete individually for research funding or to collaborate with other institutions, ERI faculty researchers have proven their strength and capability as high-performing scholars.

TABLE 2 Federal Obligations for Research and Development by Basic Carnegie Classification: 2005

Carnegie Classification 2005, Basic (survey-specific)	Federal Obligations for Research and Development
Research Universities-Very high research activity	$18,241,000
Research Universities-High research activity	$2,542,170
Doctoral/Research Universities	$433,085
Master's Colleges and Universities	$479,876
Baccalaureate Colleges	$135,019
Associate's Colleges	$32,854
Special Focus Institutions-Medical schools and medical centers	$2,678,098
Special Focus Institutions-Schools of engineering	$11,956
Special Focus Institutions-Other	$185,685
Tribal Colleges	$9,235
Not Classified	$261,762
Total	$25,010,740

NOTE: Dollar amounts are in thousands. ERIs are shaded.
SOURCE: National Science Foundation, Division of Science Resources Statistics, special tabulation.

THE IMPORTANCE OF UNDERGRADUATE RESEARCH

The impact of research on student outcomes has been studied extensively by the Council on Undergraduate Research, represented at the workshop by Kerry Karukstis, president of the Council on Undergraduate Research and professor of chemistry at Harvey Mudd College. Articles have appeared in the *Council on Undergraduate Research Quarterly* that attest to the merits of undergraduate research and emphasize the need for all institutions, regardless of size or disciplinary focus, to integrate research fully into undergraduate education. These include Wesemann (2007), Mateja (2006), Lopatto (2003), Hakim (1998), and Spilich (1997). Some of these writers reference the Boyer Commission's Report, "Reinventing Undergraduate Education" (Boyer Commission on Educating Undergraduates in the Research University, 1998 and 2002) that makes research-based learning the standard for undergraduate education for all institutions.

In the workshop, Karukstis proposed a definition for undergraduate research, as follows:

> Undergraduate research is an inquiry or investigation conducted by an undergraduate in collaboration with a faculty mentor that makes an original intellectual or creative contribution to the discipline.

This definition revisits the teacher-scholar model (Kuh et al., 2007) for faculty members and distinguishes undergraduate research from unsupervised, undirected student activity, sometimes also called research. Further, it emphasizes the fact that the scientific merit of the program must be fundamental to the undergraduate research. The student-centered nature of this process is clearly why undergraduate research has been demonstrated to be an effective pedagogical tool. However, in successful practice, it must be faculty driven, student centered, and institutionally supported.

As documented in various studies and investigations—Seymour et al. (2004), Hunter et al. (2006), and Lopatto (2006)—Karukstis then described the benefits of undergraduate research to the students who participate in it:

- Increased connection to and retention within the field
- Stronger propensity for enrollment in graduate education
- Increased employment in major-related careers
- Greater gains in academic performance and the acquisition of professional skills (cognitive adaptation, communication, interdisciplinary training)
- Greater participation in other intellectual opportunities on campus
- Increased opportunity to overcome traditional boundaries for women, minorities, and first-generation students

These findings were echoed by other presenters. Eugene Collins, director of the Division of Natural Sciences and Mathematics at Fisk University, spoke about the value of student research in teaching students about the interrelationship among the disciplines, and mentioned the increased self-confidence that students gain by being a part of a new discovery process. He cited his university's experience, where the physics department is particularly strong and where research is integral to the total academic experience. There, 50 percent of the undergraduate researchers produce a refereed journal article before graduation, thereby significantly elevating their competitiveness for acceptance to graduate school and prospective careers. This in turn strengthens the reputation of the institution and positively reinforces the students.

Benjamin Flores, the associate dean of engineering graduate studies at UTEP, articulated his institution's recent experience with undergraduate research. At their predominantly Hispanic institution, the majority of students are commuters, receive financial assistance, and are the first in their families to pursue a college degree, which makes them at risk.

Accordingly, the graduation rate[4] of students pursuing degrees in science, technology, engineering, and math (STEM) is approximately 25 percent, or half of the national average. However, among students who had a research experience, more than 90 percent completed their baccalaureate degrees at UTEP, and more than 40 percent continued on to graduate school.

Dorothy Zinsmeister, assistant vice chancellor for academic affairs for the University System of Georgia, injected the term "scholarship" rather than "research" when referring to institutional activities that produce an end product that is peer reviewed and published. In this regard, she stated that scholarship could encompass research, a view shared also by Kent Barefield, associate dean of the College of Sciences, Georgia Institute of Technology, and Jodi Wesemann of the American Chemical Society.

Near the end of the session, Marcus Shute, vice president for research and sponsored programs at Tennessee State University, contributed a quotation from Shirley Anne Jackson, the president of Rensselaer Polytechnic Institute. It emphasized the futility of trying to teach science and engineering without ever exposing the students to the underlying methodology by which these fields came to be, "Teaching without research is like confession without the sin."

ORGANIZATION OF THE REPORT

This report summarizes the presentations and discussions of the workshop under two main headings: Major Barriers to Access to Research and Solutions to Overcoming Barriers. The obstacles and solutions are presented under subheadings to enable the readers to refer to specific issues confronting the institutions.

The section "Funding and Other Resources" presents examples of the options that can be packaged to remedy the problem of limited resources. It also describes funding models that have proven effective in addressing some of the challenges facing emerging research institutions. These include federal programs that can enhance the capacity of ERIs to conduct research.

The final section synthesizes the key ideas presented by workshop participants throughout the discussion.

---

[4]Defined by the count of students graduating in six years or less from matriculation.

Barriers to Access to Research

Why can't emerging research institutions simply be transformed into robust research enterprises? For that matter, why can't their faculty successfully compete for research funding, thereby garnering the resources to encourage and sustain this significant activity? How does one initiate research in an environment that is not necessarily research friendly?

Workshop participants addressed these questions by describing the environment that illustrates the problems confronting many ERIs and citing examples.

BRANDING

There is a strong temptation to believe that while the institution's environment may not be optimal, a well-qualified, highly motivated faculty member at an ERI competes on a level playing field with research institutions for federal research funding. No one confirmed this view at the workshop. Mario Diaz (professor of physics in the Department of Physics and Astronomy and director of the Center for Gravitational Wave Astronomy at the University of Texas at Brownsville) spoke forcefully of the credibility gap that his physics research group had to constantly overcome because of peer reviewers' preconceived notions of the capabilities of his institution. The branding problem was compounded by many of the metrics expressly considered during peer review; for example, number of publications or laboratory infrastructure. Many workshop participants argued that each of these parameters reflected the institution's image as much as or more than the investigator's credentials. They felt that the use of "productivity" metrics (the absolute amount accomplished for a given stage of an investigator's career), rather than "efficiency" metrics (the amount accomplished per unit of research funding) also invariably favored researchers from research universities.

The difficulty of overcoming negative branding peppered ongoing discussions at the workshop. For example, one Historically Black College or University (HBCU) researcher spoke of her experience ghost-writing proposals for a more prominent institution. Those proposals were all funded, yet similar proposals written under her own institution's name were not funded. Another HBCU researcher spoke of the very different social reception she received when introducing herself as being from Georgetown University (one of her affiliations) versus The University of the District of Columbia (another of her affiliations).

Many participants felt that faculty at lesser-known institutions may experience the type of subtle prejudice and implicit bias described in the National Academies' *Beyond Bias and Barriers* report.[1] For example, some participants commented on the disparity between the proposal success rate of these institutions and the success rate of more well-known research institutions vis-a-vis federal agencies that fund research.

FACULTY TIME

While negative branding was described variously as annoying, discouraging, and—from time to time—patently unfair, the most concrete, insoluble problem faced by ERI researchers was identified frequently as simply the lack of time to do research. Terrence Johnson (chair of the Department of Biological Sciences at Tennessee State University) and Arlene Cole-Rhodes (associate professor of the Department of Electrical & Computer Engineering at Morgan State University) described this problem. They emphasized that teaching loads at ERIs were high, typically 3 to 4 courses a semester—about twice or three times the teaching load of a typical faculty member at a research university. Moreover, because ERIs try to ensure the greatest possible access to courses for students, classes were often taught during the day and evenings both, and included both Monday-Wednesday-Friday and Tuesday-Thursday slots. This meant there were no blocks of uninterrupted time during which to perform research.

The Johnson and Cole-Rhodes presentations pointed out that, in addition, many ERIs require their faculty to take on very serious and

[1]NAS, NAE, IOM. 2007. *Beyond Bias and Barriers: Fulfilling the Potential of Women in Academic Science and Engineering*. Washington, DC: The National Academies Press.

time-intensive student advising responsibilities. Also, any faculty member who engaged in research could count on being delegated numerous administrative duties peripherally related to the research, but required by the institution, federal law, or for professional development. These responsibilities are detailed further in the section entitled "Lack of Institutional Resources".

The presenters commented that the combination of high teaching loads, high advising loads, extra administrative duties, and limited institutional capacity for release time creates an unmanageable situation for many ERI faculty who would otherwise take an active interest in research. This is supported by a Research Corporation study of the role of research in the natural sciences at undergraduate institutions where faculty concur that the major barrier to research participation is workload.[2] The problem is that the percentage allocation of faculty time has not changed over time, although teaching and research both are more time-intensive today than in the past. The reason is that research must be continuous for it to be sustained; it can no longer be just a summer activity.

INSTITUTIONAL RESOURCES

Many ERIs have established only very limited research support units with professional staff who can provide comprehensive pre- and post-award services to faculty. Faculty who undertake research in such an environment must compensate for the lack of services that exist on campus. Following are some of the areas in which ERI researchers spoke of devoting substantial time or personal resources, in lieu of having centralized university support.

Office of Sponsored Research

Several faculty at the workshop identified themselves also as "the grants officer" for their respective projects, meaning the institution had no sponsored research office or one that was minimally staffed. These faculty members had to monitor funding opportunities and learn the intricacies of federal regulations, cost accounting procedures, conflict of interest policies, export controls, research compliance policies, the details of circulars from the U.S. Office of Management and Budget (OMB), and institutional requirements for grants submission.

Janice Cuny (NSF program director for the Broadening Participation in Computing, Computer & Information Science & Engineering Director-

[2]Research Corporation. 2002. Academic Excellence: A Study of the Role of Research in the Natural Sciences at Undergraduate Institutions. Tucson, AZ.

ate) pointed out that a thinly spread sponsored research office can cause difficulties beyond the ERIs themselves. In speaking of a multi-institution collaborative proposal, for example, Cuny noted:

> The Research I institutions would come up with subcontracts and statements of work and expect that the smaller institutions could get it signed off on in a day, and the ERIs would say, "Sorry, the only person who can sign off on that is on vacation for two weeks." There was really a mismatch of the administrative capabilities of these institutions.

At institutions with more research revenue, often it was possible to use overhead funds to support at least one grants officer, whose full-time responsibility was managing the institutional administrative responsibilities related to federally funded research programs, an allowable cost under OMB Circular A-21. One of the presenters, Karen Mitchell, director of the Office of Sponsored Projects and Research at the University of the Sciences in Philadelphia, fell into this category: a one-person sponsored research office. Yet, even one person providing research support to faculty was shown to make an incredible difference. Ms. Mitchell described how her university had been submitting five to 10 proposals a year for the 10 years prior to her being hired as the sponsored research officer. The year after she was hired, that increased to 147 applications a year. In her words, "All I had to do was make the writing and approval process easier and just really help them along the way. And that worked. It really did work."

Office of Technology Transfer

Some ERIs consider technology transfer beyond their purview. However, an NSF study prepared by Innovation Associates, Inc. argues that ERIs can be successful in this area.[3] The study presents case studies of smaller colleges and universities, including one community college, with modest research expenditures that have been successful in licensing their innovations and starting new companies. These institutions demonstrated a commitment to research, concentrated on specific research niches, hired faculty with expertise in those areas, and cultivated partnerships with local industries. Some participated in state-funded collaborative research centers and leveraged those funds to attract federal funds. The study cites the need for technology transfer and commercialization mentoring for emerging institutions.

Workshop participants acknowledged technology transfer as a

[3]Diane Palmintera. 2007. Technology Transfer and Commercialization Partnerships. Innovation Associates, Inc. under NSF Grant No. EEC-0413603.

medium for disseminating knowledge, as well as an opportunity to contribute to the economic development of the local and state community. They recognized establishment of an office of technology transfer as one of the core elements of a viable research infrastructure. Nevertheless, many commented that they are challenged by a culture on their campuses that is risk averse and not entrepreneurial, with limited research expenditures, hiring and promotion policies that do not reward technology transfer activities, and a lack of administrative support.

Business Services

One of the most heated discussions of the workshop centered on the lack of adequate business services at ERIs, combined with lengthy approvals to make use of those that do exist. According to Terrance Johnson, chair of the Department of Biological Sciences at Tennessee State University, it was nearly impossible for many purchasing or human resources departments at ERIs to deliver the resources required to support research projects in the timeframe they were needed. He spoke at length about the multiple and high-level approvals needed to accomplish certain tasks, which greatly added to the time it took for purchasing and personnel decisions. "I don't see why a requisition to purchase some sodium hydroxide has to be signed off on by a dean or a vice president for that matter," he said.

The office of physical plant at ERIs—also described as a source of problems—was able to react in the case of emergencies, but unable to conduct continuing needed maintenance, and untrained in dealing with the specialized requirements for research laboratory buildings. These advanced and ongoing efforts were left to the researcher to do personally, or to outsource through another lengthy process. Daryush Ila, professor of physics and executive director of the Alabama A&M University Research Institute, mentioned that a major benefit of establishing a research institute at Alabama A&M was the elimination of the university's many signature requirements for business processes.

After extensive discussion, Maria Thompson, associate vice president for research administration at Tennessee State University, best summarized the point:

> What I have seen happen is that the business processes will drive the academic and research enterprise versus the academic and research enterprise driving the business processes. And that's the thing I feel that really needs to change on campuses if these emerging research institutions are to move forward.

Centrally Supported Information Resources

High-performing computing and library services are considered fundamental to a university's research infrastructure. In fact, some institutions have crafted a definition of "research infrastructure" to encompass information technology in the broad range of support needed for scholarly productivity. However, workshop participants observed that services such as state-of-the-art information technology (IT) networks and libraries were rarely robust in the ERIs. The shortfall was generally covered by the researchers' time or personal investment. Arlene Cole-Rhodes discussed the problem of significant downtime in the IT system at her university, and the lack of hardware and software support. An audience member described how faculty in a certain department pool their funds to purchase library subscriptions to scientific journals as a way to address the problem of not having access to major media.

Generally, the participants acknowledged that the lack of a network that can support high-speed computation and the lack of hardware and software that can provide the required networking features (security and bandwidth) could make them less competitive for research grants. In its report, the NSF Blue Ribbon Advisory Panel on Cyberinfrastructure states the following:

> Testimony from research communities indicate that many contemporary projects require effective federation of both distributed resources (data and facilities) and distributed, multidisciplinary expertise, and that cyberinfrastructure is a key to making this possible. . . . Achieving this vision will challenge our fundamental understanding of computer and information science and engineering as well as parts of social science, and it will motivate and drive basic research in these areas.[4]

The Faculty View: Death by A Thousand Cuts

Faculty hired at ERIs sometimes knowingly accept their positions in spite of a lack of cutting-edge laboratories and impressive start-up packages. However, the extent to which institutional infrastructure impacts even the most mundane activities was visibly frustrating to many researchers who presented at the workshop. In the session presenting the faculty viewpoint, Terrance Johnson of Tennessee State University described the problems labeled as "death by a thousand cuts." These included:

[4]Revolutionizing Science and Engineering Through Cyberinfrastructure: Report of the National Science Foundation Blue-Ribbon Advisory Panel on Cyberinfrastructure, January 2003.

- Lengthy process for approvals for submitting proposals, hiring personnel, travel, and ordering materials and supplies
- Lack of or minor research start-up support such as materials and supplies, specialized equipment, travel funds, and reduced workload
- Lack of incentives and rewards such as release time, laboratory space, technical support for research programs, research awards, and salary enhancement
- Minimal provision for research program development, such as proposal development assistance, and training in locating funding prospects and proposal writing
- Lack of trained research facility maintenance staff, lengthy approvals for renovations, and too much reliance on external contracting
- Inadequate or no core facilities to decrease costs and increase competitiveness for grant awards, and no standard protocols for the use of core facilities
- Lack of investment in professional development for post-award grants officers, and ineffective post-award communication with principal investigators
- Inefficient business support processes such as purchasing and receiving and deliveries
- Inadequate support for library acquisitions

Arlene Cole-Rhodes of Morgan State University commented on the problem of inadequate publication support for faculty submitting papers to journals; e.g., clerical assistance to ease the burden of reformatting a paper according to a journal's specifications once a paper is accepted for publication. She added that this lack of support affects the publication acceptance rate for faculty at ERIs.

FACULTY REWARD SYSTEM

In *Scholarship Reconsidered*, Boyer (1990) challenged universities to adopt a new paradigm for defining scholarly activity to include the scholarship of integration, the scholarship of application, and the scholarship of teaching, replacing the traditional definitions of research.[5] In revising their tenure policies to embrace this concept, some institutions have fallen short of implementing these principles systematically. Experts agree that the faculty reward system must be congruent with the mission and vision of the institution; see, for example O'Meara (2006) and Diamond (1999). Thus, workshop participants observed that as ERIs shift to greater empha-

[5]Ernest L. Boyer. 1990. Scholarship Reconsidered: Priorities of the Professoriate. Stanford, CA: Carnegie Foundation for the Advancement of Teaching.

sis on research, they must institute faculty reward structures that validate that commitment while reflecting the synergy of teaching and research.

The rewards and incentives discussed at the workshop included a more flexible release time policy, better balance in faculty evaluations of emphasis on research versus teaching, start-up funds, research venture capital, returned overhead from grants (to further support the principal investigator's research), and advocacy for the researchers themselves. Some also commented that faculty course loads must be adjusted for research mentoring as a routine activity.

Researchers in teaching-intensive environments often are in competition for space, tenure and promotion, and teaching loads with their fellow faculty who were not pursuing research. Though not an explicit topic of the workshop, the discussion around reward systems emerged sufficiently often that the issue merits a place in this report.

Solutions to Overcoming Barriers: Strategic Partnerships for Economies of Scale

STRATEGIC APPROACHES

The second half of the workshop presented potential solutions for the problems already described; namely, lack of time for faculty to do research, lack of institutional resources, and an inadequate reward system. The solutions shared several commonalities, or strategic intents. One was the willingness to embrace dynamism at the university; to change structures, systems, and processes so that these could evolve in a manner required to promote a culture of research.

A second strategic intent was the dogged pursuit of resources. In the case of services that needed to be provided (sponsored research office, business services, technology transfer, grants management), the solution often meant partnering with an organization that already had the necessary functions at a significant scale, and then using the partner's economies of scale to achieve the needed functions at a reduced price. In the case of cash needs (e.g., startup packages, salary improvements, new equipment), resources often had to be found via grant applications to state and federal agencies, internal reallocations, or more intensive fundraising from private sources. The process of first identifying a need and then tenaciously pursuing external resources was a powerful method of initiating everything from technology transfer offices to faculty "reassigned" time. (Refer to the recommendations of Marcus Shute, Tennessee State University, in Box 1). The converse—pursuing resources without regard to the specific needs they were required fill—was not recommended by any of the presenters at the workshop. Instead, most participants agreed

BOX 1
Recommendations for ERIs to Expand and Strengthen Research Resources

- Tennessee Board of Regents (TBR) and State of Tennessee must offer competitive compensation at all levels to attract and retain researchers, faculty, and staff.
- Implement interdisciplinary proposal development groups centered around various research themes to stimulate collaboration and assist junior faculty.
- Develop a strategy to increase the number of new faculty and researchers annually and provide competitive start-up funding in targeted areas.
- Include the Division of Research on the committee for faculty recruitment; ensure there is a research orientation in the faculty hiring process.
- Nurture new research faculty and provide some support during summer for at least two summers; provide mentoring opportunities with senior faculty that are research-active.
- State of Tennessee should invest in research infrastructure (buildings, labs, equipment, etc.) at institutions that have demonstrated expertise and research proficiency.
- Incorporate research metrics, i.e., funding and publications, into tenure award and promotion process.
- Develop and revise guidelines (University and TBR) for faculty teaching load requirement; i.e., build some release time into full load requirement for research program development.
- Enhance TBR strategies to promote collaboration, expertise, and capacity building (human, technological, facilities, etc.), and adequacy of resources for research at TBR institutions. This includes recruitment, retention, and sustainability of current research infrastructure.
- Actively promote multi-state and international research collaboration and exposure of TBR research capability.

Presented by Marcus Shute, vice president for research, Tennessee State University.

that ERIs should develop a road map, including metrics to gauge progress for evolving to some desired state of research productivity, and target resources to enable the accomplishment of that goal (see Appendix E).

The presentations by Benjamin Flores (UTEP—University of Texas, El Paso) and Mario Diaz (UTB—University of Texas, Brownsville) articulated another strategy common among those institutions that had achieved steep growth rates in their research portfolios, including UTEP, UTB, and Alabama A&M. This was, that growth was possible but required targeted investments in a few faculty within a subset of departments. UTEP was an exemplar in this respect, having grown from a research funding base

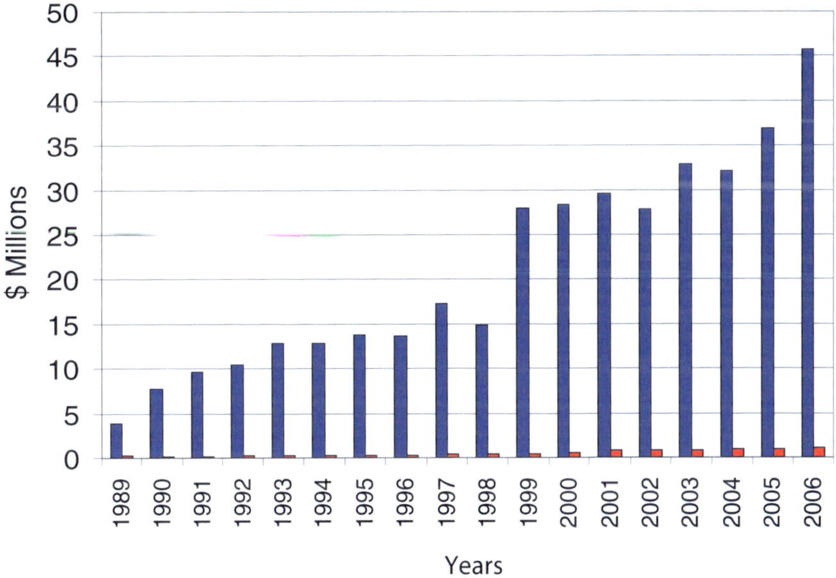

FIGURE 3 University of Texas at El Paso, history of research expenditures.
NOTE: Total research expenditures and expenditures on research infrastructure.
SOURCE: College of of Engineering, UTEP.

of about $4 million in 1989 to more than $45 million in 2006, largely through the activities of the Colleges of Education, Science, and Engineering (Figure 3). Flores noted that 50 percent of UTEP's research funding was the result of just 17 people, and so supporting those 17 individuals with effective administrative procedures, "reassigned time," and tangible rewards was critical to the growth of the university in its research endeavors. Those individuals' ability to raise funds then paved the way for the next generation of incoming researchers, in the same college, to enter a more research-intensive environment with more robust resources. This strategy allows emerging research institutions to focus on areas in which they are particularly well-suited by virtue of geography, access to special populations, prominent alumni, or unusual faculty expertise; thus making success more likely.

These three approaches—embracing dynamism, finding or sharing other resources, and targeted investment of the resources at hand—are illustrated by the solutions that follow.

FACULTY TIME

- **Consolidate Many Small Classes into Fewer Large Ones**

One solution to the lack of faculty research time identified at the workshop is to have faculty teach fewer classes. While many ERIs pride themselves on a small student-to-teacher ratio, this strategy necessitates having one professor teach multiple small sections of the same course. However, this practice significantly increases faculty teaching load.

Dorothy Zinsmeister, assistant vice chancellor for academic affairs for the University System of Georgia, explained what happened when, as a department chair at Kennesaw State University, she increased class sizes. Her plan had been to consolidate three classes with 30 students into one class with 90 to 120 students, thereby decreasing the teaching load for the professor from 15 to 18 hours per week to 4 to 7 hours per week. As she described it, there was substantial hesitation from the faculty with regard to the proposed plan:

> Part of that reluctance had to do with their perception that we were going to change student performance, that grades were going to go down because you were in this one . . . cozy little classroom of 21 students where you knew everybody's name and could give students more attention. You were now in a big lecture room and classroom, and students were not going to do as well as they did. And then they were also concerned about the effects on faculty evaluations.

To deal with this skepticism, Zinsmeister created four sections of different sizes for one of the introductory courses in Fall 2000. After the semester was over, she gathered data on student performance as a function of class size. The sections with 21, 60, 99, and 110 students yielded class GPAs of 2.47, 2.91, 2.47, and 2.81, respectively. In other words, there was no systematic impact of class size on student performance as measured by GPA.

This was confirmed by an analysis of trends at the same institution over a period of time. Over the course of seven years, the ability to teach more students in fewer large classes increased the credit hours earned from the department from 2,856 to 5,956 for the course in question. This provided additional revenue to the department. Faculty research activities with students increased dramatically from one to about seven projects per year. Faculty publications increased by about 50 percent in the same time period, as did sponsored research awards.

- **Make Research an Undergraduate Class**

For institutions in which it is not easy to trade teaching time directly for research time, Zinsmeister showed that it is sometimes possible to achieve the same end by formulating one's research project as a small project-oriented undergraduate class. The professor's research activity then is labeled "teaching" by the system and substitutes for one of the classes the professor is otherwise required to teach. University resources allocated to classroom teaching also then become accessible to the professor for research. The undergraduate research class is also a very direct way to encourage undergraduate engagement in research.

- **Consolidate Teaching Schedules**

As previously mentioned (and as originally noted by Terrance Johnson), the indiscriminate distribution of teaching obligations between day and evenings, throughout the Monday-Wednesday-Friday cycle *and* the Tuesday-Thursday cycle can leave faculty with no blocks of time large enough to pursue research. Better thought-out consolidation of faculty schedules is therefore one tool for opening up time for research.

- **Provide "Reassigned Time" (Release Time)**

The practice of using research funding to pay for a teaching substitute is usually termed "release time." It is a direct means of creating time for research. Dorothy Zinsmeister used the alternative term "reassigned time" to reflect the fact that the time is not free but is reallocated from teaching to research. While this is common in research institutions, thereby making their relatively low teaching loads even lower, it is harder to implement in ERIs. In addition to Zinsmeister, presenters Diaz (UTB), Flores (UTEP), Johnson (TSU), and Cole-Rhodes (Morgan State) each mentioned the need to implement some form of reassigned time to enable research. Two of the presenters, Johnson and Diaz, mentioned the need repeatedly.

Ben Flores pointed out that reassigned time for new faculty—those who most need the time to launch research, but do not yet have the research funding to support teaching relief—was painfully difficult for the institution to absorb. No funding models other than the use of the university's own funds were presented for solving the problem of how to support reassigned time for faculty who did not yet have research grants.

Several participants expressed their inability to arrange for reassigned time even when money was plentiful. Alan Gabrielli, dean of the School of Arts and Sciences at Southern Polytechnic State University, said, ". . . for colleagues at other universities around the state, a constant complaint was that no matter how much money the system gave them to find replacement faculty, they just couldn't do it." Existing faculty were often so thinly spread as not to have a duplicate content expert on campus who could teach the researcher's class. Substitute instructors from nearby institutions also were hard to find, either because of geographic isolation or a lack of relationships among peer institutions. Partnerships that aggregated potential teaching replacements among multiple institutions were a potential solution, but one not elucidated further at the workshop.

- **Implement Faculty Sabbaticals at Research Universities**

The problem of finding time to do research is greatly minimized if the ERI researcher can spend a semester or year in a research university, teaching only one course and gaining access to the many extant support structures for research: research-active colleagues, technical libraries, IT support, technicians, grant-processing offices, state-of-the-art laboratory equipment, post-doctoral students, etc. This experience is particularly valuable for ERI faculty who wish to launch research programs at their home institutions on return, because they are better positioned to compete for grant awards that may support additional reassigned and release time for research.

Jim Muyskens (former senior vice chancellor for academic affairs for the University System of Georgia and currently president of Queens College, CUNY) described how the University System of Georgia, using state funding, launched a program to provide ERI researchers a semester or year at the Georgia Institute of Technology. This faculty development program operated for several years until state budgets were dramatically reduced in the aftermath of post-dot.com budget shortages in 2000 and 2001 when hundreds of start-up businesses on the Internet crashed. Muyskens presented several anecdotes about successful, long-term research collaborations and continuing publication streams generated by the program's early participants.

Kent Barefield (associate dean, College of Sciences, Georgia Institute of Technology), who managed this program at Georgia Tech, mentioned that the program's attractiveness to both ERI researchers and their Georgia Tech hosts could be attributed partly to the program's funding paradigm. The sending institution, the receiving institution, and the program participants all benefitted as follows:

- Funds were given to the ERI to assist in hiring a replacement instructor.
- Housing allowances were given to ERI participants to allow them to move to Atlanta.

• Funds were given to Georgia Tech for the ERI researcher to use while conducting research at Georgia Tech.

• Start-up funds (small) were given to the ERI researcher to use in launching a research program on return to his or her home institution.

Muyskens and Barefield concluded by pointing out that Georgia's Faculty Development Program yielded lasting benefits to Georgia Tech, as well as to the ERIs, including:

• Better preparation of ERI students transferring to Georgia Tech. The returning ERI faculty member brought a clearer understanding of the subject matter mastered by Georgia Tech students and could redesign courses at the ERI accordingly.

• Improved teaching in some Georgia Tech classes. Many of the ERI faculty had extensive teaching experience and were able to implement lasting pedagogical innovations at Georgia Tech. One ERI program participant's students won campus writing awards.

• Use Faculty Development to Optimize Use of the Limited Time Available for Research

Given the time pressures on ERI faculty, research efficiency is a must. Increased efficiency can be achieved through faculty development programs, either formal or informal. The Georgia Faculty Development Program described above is an example of a formal program. Maria Thompson also described the Proposal Development Groups that were launched at Tennessee State University (see Box 2). Small groups of senior faculty meet in groups with junior faculty in the same or similar fields and engage in a number of research support activities. Each group has a facilitator who, in return for their service to the university, receives support staff and funds for activities such as external reviews of large institutional proposals.

The program is relatively new, but the Tennessee State Division of Research and Sponsored Programs intends to expand it further by bringing speakers to the campus and offering other enrichment events. Morgan State also has a faculty mentoring program, according to Arlene Cole-Rhodes.

Lunchtime discussions revealed that, in some institutions, the group mentoring concept has been extended to include learning communities of peer mentors as well. For example, the National Science Foundation (NSF), represented at the workshop by Janice Cuny, has been able to extend the faculty development concept across institutions with its STARS Alliance. Here, faculty from multiple institutions regularly share best

BOX 2
Functions of Proposal Development Groups—
Tenessee State University

- Research mentoring which is an acceptable activity in each participant's faculty development plan
- A forum to discuss research ideas and review proposals prior to deadlines
- Guidance on selection of funding announcements
- Uniform and meaningful analysis of relevant institutional data required for proposals
- Advice on the development of internal and external partnerships
- Coordination of student researchers
- Support in peripheral requirements for successful proposals such as assistance with budget development
- Professional formatting and layout of documents

practices in curriculum development, research, and mentoring in meetings. In addition, the STARS program provides support for students for service learning projects in computer science, thereby engaging students directly in applying their knowledge.

Workshop participants suggested that professional expertise also can be gained rapidly by volunteering to serve on proposal review panels at federal agencies. The NSF, in particular, allows individuals to self-nominate to serve on review panels in their field.

INSTITUTIONAL RESOURCES

As mentioned earlier, the lack of support services at ERIs can all but cripple the ability to conduct research and a university's ability to manage federal programs. Below are some of the solutions proposed at the workshop to deliver services in key areas.

Office of Sponsored Research

For those institutions that have no sponsored research office, it is sometimes possible to partner with a research institution to provide pre- and post-award services. The partnership can be improved if there are mutual rewards. Susan Ross, director of the Office for Sponsored Research at Northwestern University, Evanston Campus, and Adam Kessel, education developer at the American Indian Center of Chicago, described the case of a successful partnership among Northwestern, the East-West University, and the American Indian Center on an NSF project to build capacity to do cutting-edge research in a Native American community. The project was designed to examine the cultural context of Native American science education.

To obtain the grant, the Northwestern provost had to commit his sponsored research office to assisting the partner institutions, which had never processed a proposal for a federal grant. What followed was a hands-on approach, with Northwestern walking its ERI colleagues through new awardee forms, cash management processes, FastLane submissions, report writing, regulatory policies and procedures, and more. In turn, the ERI colleagues educated Northwestern officials about influential cultural norms; for example, the fact that the entire tribe had to approve a project before it could be implemented. Each partner received a separate NSF grant award.

The principal investigator at Northwestern reported that "this kind of collaboration does a lot to move the university toward its goal of increasing diversity." Another benefit to Northwestern of the administrative collaboration is the ability to promote its relationship with indigenous communities. The benefit to the ERIs includes cross-generational community involvement around issues of STEM education. The most powerful outcome has been greater interest by tribe members in research and education, with many deciding to pursue baccalaureate or advanced degrees as a result of the project, including high school drop-outs who are now returning to school. Of course, the Native American institutions now have the capability to begin managing some of their own federal grants and have received new grants in turn.

In one of the final presentations of the day, the workshop participants learned of the Federal Demonstration Partnership (FDP), a membership organization dedicated to streamlining the administrative burden related to research. Because the FDP counts federal agency representatives among its members, its meeting agendas offer very timely insights into upcoming changes in federal grant requirements and procedures. The organization recently launched an Emerging Research Institutions group, and was described as an excellent environment for ERI research administrators to learn the latest news and state-of-the-art practices from both federal program officers and peer administrators in research and emerging research institutions.

Office of Technology Transfer

Emerging Research Institutions may have few researchers, but some of these are highly entrepreneurial. As the research administration infrastructure evolves, principal investigators will begin to ask about securing patents and copyrights. Technology transfer, however, is viewed as an unaffordable luxury and is one of the last bastions of resistance to research. In addition, because a technology transfer office is not a profit center in many institutions, it is doubly hard for ERIs to justify this internal expenditure. Several extrinsic solutions were discussed at the workshop.

One option is to partner with an institution that already has a robust tech transfer operation. This was the approach taken by the University of the Sciences in Philadelphia (USP), whose researchers were active in pharmacology and needed to patent their drug discoveries and drug delivery inventions. Karen Mitchell, director of the Office of Sponsored Projects and Research, described how USP first obtained a state grant to establish its own tech transfer office, but found there was no post-grant funding mechanism that would make it possible to hire permanent, qualified personnel to staff the office. When the first grant expired, the university was reduced once again to using expensive outside attorneys for their occasional but growing tech transfer needs. A breakthrough came with the second grant, which was used to form a partnership with Thomas Jefferson University (TJU). USP would establish an Office of Intellectual Property using existing personnel, while TJU would actively mentor those personnel until they became experts, and would provide technical assistance to USP in technology transfer processing matters. Moreover, all licensing activity would be handled by TJU in exchange for a portion of the licensing revenue. USP now has an Office of Intellectual Property and is able to actively provide a full suite of technology transfer services to the faculty.

A second approach to the dilemma of how to provide tech transfer services to ERI faculty is outsourcing. As an example, Tanaga Boozer described the capabilities of Intellectual Property Solutions, a small company that provides a virtual tech transfer office to universities that may not be in a position to establish their own. She commented that because intellectual property is an intangible asset, it is particularly well suited to virtual solutions.

Business Services

Business services, particularly human resource and procurement functions, were clearly a frustration for many ERI researchers. ERI campuses failed to have such systems robust enough to handle the demands and timetables associated with managing a research enterprise. A few individuals such as Marcus Shute of Tennessee State mentioned their university's progress in streamlining these processes internally. However, an attractive option for researchers in less nimble institutions might be to outsource the post-award functions entirely. Daryush Ila of Alabama

A&M stressed the benefits of setting up a research institute, inside of which all procurement and personnel functions could be handled separately from the university-based processes in these categories, and more efficiently as well.

Janet Polli, an associate at the Research Foundation of the City University of New York (CUNY), described the GrantsPlus program at the Foundation as a viable alternative to establishing a post-award administrative office. The creation of GrantsPlus was inspired by the Research Foundation's success in distributing 9/11 funds to more than 10,000 individual recipients. Confident that they had the capacity and automation to serve institutions beyond their 23 CUNY campuses, the Research Foundation established GrantsPlus as a separate, non-profit organization that could provide post-award processing to other non-profits throughout the nation. The web-based systems facilitate fiscal management and reporting, sponsor liaison and compliance management, payroll, fringe benefit administration, vendor payments, time and leave tracking, and more. The fee for the service is a small percentage of grant expenditures and can be written into a grant as a valid direct or indirect cost. Expenses are monitored against the grant terms and conditions, as well as against the approved budget. Financial reports are updated several times daily, in near real-time. The Research Foundation currently processes more than $360 million in government grants for the CUNY schools. For participating institutions, obviating the need to operate their own post-award processing system can enable them to realize significant cost-savings.

Centrally Supported Information Resources

In the first half of the workshop, participants discussed two needs in the area of information resources: robust IT networks and more extensive journal access. No solutions to the first problem were identified in the workshop, but the GALILEO project, described by Merryll Penson, executive director of library services, University System of Georgia, was offered as a model for solving the problem of access to journal subscriptions.

GALILEO (Georgia Library Learning Online) is a statewide virtual library and an initiative of the Board of Regents of the University System of Georgia. GALILEO is currently accessible to over 2,000 institutions—public schools, public and private universities, technical colleges, public libraries, and private K-12 schools in Georgia. Seventy-eight of these institutions are academic libraries, 35 public and 43 private. GALILEO therefore provides access to its 8,000 journal subscriptions to virtually every library in the state.

The GALILEO staff negotiates contracts for databases, maintains and improves the web interface that delivers them, provides a universal catalogue and universal borrowing system (for USG libraries), offers 24-hour helpdesk support, and coordinates special purchases between and among libraries in Georgia. Bulk buying power and centralized support make GALILEO extremely cost competitive compared to maintaining electronic subscriptions at individual libraries. Albany State University (an HBCU), for example, nearly halved the number of its journal subscriptions after the introduction of GALILEO.

The funding for GALILEO originally came from state lottery money, but over time the funding has shifted to state funds. Private academic libraries and schools pay fees to participate. GALILEO also facilitates group purchases to secure holdings not currently covered in the core set of 8,000 journals.

At present, Georgia is one of several states providing universal library access through state funding. The culture of the state determines the particular participants and holdings. Others states with similar programs include Ohio (OhioLink), North Carolina (NC LIVE) and Virginia (VIVA).

FACULTY REWARD SYSTEM

Given the hurdles facing ERI researchers, several audience members as well as presenters stressed the importance of ensuring there were adequate rewards. Four reward types were discussed: flexible tenure policy, start-up funds, returned overhead/research incentives, and reassigned time. Reassigned time was discussed earlier, but the suggested solutions for the remaining three items are discussed here.

Flexible Tenure Policy

Fortunately, because tenure is primarily a policy issue more than a financial issue, it can be one of the easier changes to implement on an ERI campus to encourage research. Ben Flores of UTEP stressed the importance of revisiting tenure and promotion guidelines so that research is emphasized more in tenure decisions, saying. "Tenure and promotion decisions play a crucial role in retaining outstanding faculty." Jim Muyskens mentioned that the University System of Georgia (where he had been a senior vice chancellor) had, in addition, implemented post-tenure review with criteria specific to research, and that this practice had in fact been what motivated some of the ERI faculty in the University System of Georgia to begin to look at retooling themselves through faculty development programs. Dorothy Zinsmeister (University System of Georgia) confirmed the system's insistence on post-tenure review in some form and referred audience members to their web site for the state-wide policy. For example, at USG, the reviews are performed at the level of the individual and the chair, meaning each department or school can set its own criteria for success in teaching and research.

Start-Up Funds

If an emerging research institution finds itself in the position of having an excellent department that is poised to be a premier department—competing on an equal footing with departments at the research universities—the ability to create attractive start-up packages for star junior faculty becomes a pressing issue. Mario Diaz (UTB) pointed out that the physics department at the University of Texas, Brownsville, now finds itself in this position and has no mechanisms by which to provide the financing for such packages. Unattractive though it may be, it appeared that the only real solution was to reroute internal university funds from other areas. Terrance Johnson (TSU) commented on the complete inadequacy of start-up packages in the $10,000 range. For universities not used to the cost of research, $10,000 might seem like substantial funding, but it is about an order of magnitude below the cost of a single piece of equipment: "We need administrators who realize that science is expensive."

Returned Overhead and Research Incentives

Terrance Johnson (TSU) first brought up the topic of returned overhead, or other research incentive awards. Common in research universities, this practice takes a small portion of the grant-generated overhead dollars and returns it to the researcher for use in furthering his or her research. According to Vijaya Melnick (director of the Office of Sponsored Research and Programs at the University of the District of Columbia), the practice is not so common in ERIs. She said, "Many universities don't make use of the indirect cost allocation as research incentives." This kind of incentive system requires a small sacrifice by the university, but is disproportionately appreciated by researchers, who are given more flexibility in managing their research as a result.

FUNDING AND OTHER RESOURCES

The need to find resources was an imperative for most of the innovations presented at the workshop. Resources were not easily found, but did exist. The workshop featured four sources of support as examples of programs available through federal agencies: the Army's Mentor-Protégé program, NIH's Extramural Associates Research and Development Award (EARDA) at the Child Health and Human Development Institute, the NSF

STARS Alliance, and the Experimental Program to Stimulate Competitive Research program (EPSCoR). The last of these is offered across multiple agencies.

U.S. Army Mentor-Protégé Program

Tracey Pinson, director of the Office of Small Business Programs, Department of the Army, presented numerous options for ERIs to become involved in Army procurements. She described the suite of research and development programs offered by the Army command centers and the Corps of Engineers, and she mentioned that the primary vehicle for doing business is contracts, which is an impediment for many ERIs.

She referenced the Department of Defense (DoD) small business goal of awarding 5 percent of the total contracts awarded to all higher education institutions to HBCUs and other minority institutions (MIs). DoD includes HBCUs and MIs in its definition of small disadvantaged businesses for the purpose of reporting progress toward achieving the 5 percent goal. She reported, however, that the Army exceeds that goal annually by awarding 20 percent of its procurements to those institutions, excluding awards to federally funded research centers or university-affiliated research centers.

Pinson discussed three programs that she thought are relevant for ERIs: the Small Business Innovation Research Program (SBIR), Small Business Technology Transfer Program (STTR), and Mentor-Protégé Program.

The Mentor-Protégé Program particularly resonated with the workshop participants. In describing the program, Pinson mentioned that the Army provides funding for large companies to mentor small disadvantaged businesses (includes HBCUs and MIs) in the area of government contracting. Successful mentoring companies not only have all mentoring expenses reimbursed, but are eligible for awards and for extra points in competition for DOD contracts.

For many ERIs, government contracting is a specialty skill whose absence on campus precludes ERI researchers from accepting large DOD contracts, or contracts from other agencies. The ability to obtain contracting expertise through mentoring would present a significant opportunity for ERIs' ability to secure research funding and to develop long-term collaborations for future joint efforts.

Unfortunately, the Mentor-Protégé Program is legislatively constrained from having universities serve as mentors. Pinson stated it was "number one on my list" to recommend changes in the legislation to permit universities to participate as mentors as well as protégés. She mentioned that DOD had some technical assistance programs to assist institutions with contracting basics, and that these were already in place.

Some workshop participants noted that the Department of Energy (DOE) also has a mentor-protégé program with similar eligibility requirements. The difference is that DOE does not fund the partnerships directly. Instead, "they expect the research dollars that go to their facilities, particularly research labs, to create these mentor–protégé agreements and partnerships as part of their research programs. This arrangement provides great opportunities for the schools, and it is a true partnership."

NIH Extramural Associates Program

The Program Director of NIH's Extramural Associates Program, Regina James, was not available to give a presentation about the program, and Jean Flagg Newton, the cognizant program officer, substituted in this capacity. She described the mission of the office as follows:

> [to] increase research capacity, training and outreach at minority serving institutions and women's colleges and expand global research infrastructure that will lead to diverse contributions to biomedical and behavioral research.

She then described the program's primary award, the Extramural Associates Research and Development Award (EARDA) as, "[a] comprehensive approach to establishing research infrastructure and providing the appropriate training that will allow institutions to contribute to research."

The domestic EARDA award targets women's colleges and institutions serving minorities. The award provides $70,000 a year for five years, primarily allocated to strengthening research administration infrastructure. The award provides staff training that focuses on NIH policies and procedures, grants management, and knowledge of federal and nonfederal funding opportunities. In addition, it supports staff and training in research administration, the creation of databases, collaborative opportunities with other institutions, and workshops on research ethics.

The EARDA program sponsors the creation of pilot research projects (up to $40,000 in the fourth and fifth years of the grant) and professional development activities, including technical assistance workshops in grantsmanship and research methodologies. These activities are designed to enhance knowledge related to the development of competitive research grant applications, as well as provide networking opportunities among colleagues.

NSF STAR Alliance and the Experimental Program to Stimulate Competitive Research

STAR Alliance is one of three categories of awards under the NSF Broadening Participation in Computing (BPC) program. Janice Cuny, BPC program director, described the types of alliances that are enabled by the STAR Alliance projects. She highlighted the fact that the projects have created partnerships across institutional types that aim to broaden the participation of underrepresented groups in the computing disciplines. They also have enhanced the research and educational capacity at the research institutions and ERI members of the alliance. The Alliances stimulate curricular reform, research experiences for undergraduates, and peer team research for partnering institutions. However, in order to compete successfully for a grant award, the proposers must have a strong organization and management plan.

Denise Barnes of the Office of Integrative Activities presented information about the NSF Experimental Program to Stimulate Competitive Research (EPSCoR). EPSCoR funds are dedicated to the advancement of research and education in jurisdictions receiving lesser amounts of NSF research funding. The program currently encompasses 25 states as well as the Commonwealth of Puerto Rico and the U.S. Virgin Islands.

Because the program is congressionally mandated across a number of agencies, the NSF presentation was but one example of the types of assistance offered under the program. EPSCoR offers research infrastructure improvement grants (up to $3 million annually), joint support of proposals submitted through other NSF channels, and a variety of outreach and workshop events to familiarize EPSCoR researchers with NSF programs, priorities, and policies.

THE FUNDING MODELS

The Mentor-Protégé, EARDA, STAR Alliance, and EPSCoR programs are but four examples of federal resources available to ERIs wishing to enhance their research capacity and infrastructure. But these four examples also illustrate a more general fact: the resources available to ERIs are highly targeted to specific populations, regions, or entities.

Unfortunately, the lack of research infrastructure is a universal condition of many ERIs. While scientific equipment may be obtained by a sole researcher with a terrific grant proposal and luck on his or her side, the systemic upgrading of facilities and processes remains a universal problem without universal support. The fact that capacity-building programs, particularly at the federal level, are not correspondingly universal makes them difficult even to locate. Only three of the workshop attendees indicated they had heard of the Army or NIH programs. The most powerful argument for retaining the restrictions on eligibility was that the funding levels—at least for the programs presented in the workshop—were not large enough to support a fully open, nationwide set of programs.

On the other hand, not all of the restrictions are rational. One participant noted that Dartmouth, a research university, is eligible for EPSCoR funding now that New Hampshire has been declared an EPSCoR state. The lack of universal access does mean that these programs are unavailable to a large percentage of the 70 percent or so of the nation's students who are not in doctorate-granting universities.

Despite the dearth of widely available opportunities through federal agencies, other approaches to enhancing the administrative infrastructure were mentioned throughout the workshop as well. These strategies are summarized in Table 3 below, along with the federal programs described above.

TABLE 3 Resources for Research-Enhancing Initiatives

Source	Sample ERI Strategy
State legislature	Galileo project (USG)
University system	Faculty Development Program (USG)
Private foundations and organizations	Office of Intellectual Property (USP)
Federal agencies	
NSF STAR Alliance	Partnerships across institutional types
NSF EPSCoR	Faculty and student research collaboration
NSF PREM	Research training and professional development
NSF MSP and LSAMP	
NIH MORE Programs	Mentoring
NIH EARDA	Technical assistance
Army and DOE Mentor-Protégé	Grantsmanship workshops
SBIR and STTR	
Outsourcing	Grants Plus
	Intellectual Property Solutions
Partnerships	Sponsored programs administration
	Technology transfer functions
	Regulatory compliance support
	Staff training
	Research capacity building
Internal funding	Start-up funds
	Research awards
	Return of overhead receipts
	Research incentives for new research projects

Summary

Several points summarize the workshop discussions.

Most workshop participants said repeatedly that emerging research institutions can develop a "research culture" and embrace the broad connotation of the term—adopting some of the principles proposed by Lee Shulman (president of The Carnegie Foundation for the Advancement of Teaching) regarding the scholarship of teaching and learning. For example, they can offer courses that sufficiently empower students by imparting the knowledge and skills needed to conduct research and to successfully complete graduate programs. Such courses also can demonstrate the interconnection between research and education and can help to institutionalize undergraduate research. As Terry Millar, professor of mathematics at the University of Wisconsin-Madison, stated, "In order to understand the discipline, doing research is just part of the game to get the mentality of what the arguments are." ERIs also can place more emphasis on research as a factor in faculty evaluations and afford recognition and special awards for research accomplishments, including undergraduate research.

> *The rest of the world is shifting bases. And I think that faculty, both in research universities and small universities, will have to undergo what amounts to a paradigm shift in the way they work and think. And we have to start with research behavior.* (Workshop Participant)

Many participants emphasized that administrative leadership can be pivotal in developing a research climate. Leadership is needed to stimulate internal collaboration in order to leverage resources and provide access and opportunity for research experiences to larger numbers of students. In addition, it enables researchers to share their findings and promotes more interdisciplinary activities. ERIs can develop "learning communities" especially for junior faculty where there is not a critical mass of disciplinary expertise in one department. In that model, young faculty members would not be embedded in older departments with most of the faculty already tenured. They would, instead, be able to find the synergy needed to incubate and nurture innovative ideas.

Administrators must be better informed about the value and cost of doing research, as a number of participants emphasized. Realistic estimates of expenditures needed for research support personnel, materials, and equipment will help guide decisions about research investments. Realistically, developing a research enterprise is difficult and expensive. However, good strategic planning and investment can optimize the results and minimize the liabilities.

Many participants stressed the need for ERIs to provide seed capital for emerging and potentially productive research areas that could increase their capacity to compete. They stated that the institutions also should provide attractive start-up packages to recruit bright experimental scientists and young investigators to enable them to become productive, high-performing researchers.

Marcus Shute commented that ERIs could appeal to state legislatures, federal agencies, and foundations for funding to propel these institutions into more competitive research enterprises. He added that they should encourage federal agencies to provide grant programs to enable minority-serving institutions to develop the critical mass of research talent needed (UT-Brownsville and UT-El Paso models) to support the nation's scientific and technological foundation. Programs such as the NSF Math and Science Partnership and Louis Stokes Alliance for Minority Participation have helped institutions such as UTEP to achieve research-intensive status. Research is important enough to the educational enterprise that some mechanism, such as a variation of the EPSCoR model, could be explored to competitively fund research at the institutions that serve the majority of students who are underrepresented in the STEM disciplines.

Workshop participants reiterated that collaboration and partnerships among ERIs, research institutions, and other organizations can offer solutions to the infrastructure impediments to research. They echoed the sentiment that research and education are not mutually exclusive, particularly in the context of educating the future workforce, and that ERIs should exploit the resources that can enable them to reach the next level of institutional enterprise development. The participants noted that "strategic" is the operative term in forming partnerships so that ERIs can market their intellectual assets effectively.

References

Boyer, E.L. (1990). Scholarship Reconsidered: Priorities of the Professoriate. The Carnegie Foundation for the Advancement of Teaching: Stanford, CA.

Boyer Commission on Educating Undergraduates in the Research University. Reinventing Undergraduate Education: A Blueprint for America's Research Universities, Princeton, NJ: The Carnegie Foundation; 1998 and Boyer Revisited, 2002. Retrieved from *http://naples.cc.suny.edu/pres/boyer.nsf/.*

Diamond, R.M. (1999). *Aligning Faculty Rewards with Institutional Mission: Statements, Policies, and Guidelines*. Bolton, MA Anker.

Hakim, T. (1998). Soft Assessment of Undergraduate Research Reactions and Student Perspectives, *Council on Undergraduate Research Quarterly* 18:189-192.

Hauger, J.S. and McEnaney, C. Eds.(2000). *Strategies for Competitiveness in Academic Research.* Committee on Science, Engineering, and Public Policy, American Association for the Advancement of Science: Washington, DC.

Hunter, A.-B., Laurensen, S.L., and Seymour, E. (2006). Becoming a Scientist: The Role of Undergraduate Research in Students' Cognitive, Personal, and Professional Development. *Science Education* 91:36-74.

Kuh, G.D., Chen, D. and Laird, T.F.N. (2007). Why Teacher-Scholars Matter. Some Insights from FSSE and NSSE. *Liberal Education* 93:40-45.

Lopatto, D. (2003). The Essential Features of Undergraduate Research, *Council on Undergraduate Research Quarterly* 24:139-142.

Lopatto, D. (2006). Undergraduate Research as a Catalyst for Liberal Learning. *Peer Review* 8:22-25.

Mateja, J. (2006). Undergraduate Research: Needed More Today Than Ever Before, *Council on Undergraduate Research Quarterly* 27:27-32.

National Science Foundation. (2008). Science and Engineering Indicators, NSF: Arlington, VA.

O'Meara, K. (2006). Encouraging Multiple Forms of Scholarship in Faculty Reward Systems: Have Academic Cultures Really Changed? *New Directions for Institutional Research* 129:77-95.

Research Corporation. (2002). Academic Excellence: A Study of the Role of Research in the Natural Sciences at Undergraduate Institutions. Tucson, AZ.

Seymour, E., Hunter, A-B., Laurensen, S.L., and DeAntoni, T. (2004). Establishing the Benefits of Research Experiences for Undergraduates: First Findings from a Three-Year Study. *Science Education* 88:493-534.

Spilich, G. (1997). Does Undergraduate Research Pay Off? *Council on Undergraduate Research Quarterly* 18:57-59, 89.

Wesemann, J. (2007). Making the Case for Undergraduate Research: Focus on U.S. Competitiveness, *Council on Undergraduate Research Quarterly* 28:38-40.

Appendixes

Appendix A

Committee Member Biographies

JULIET GARCIA (*Chair*), is President of the University of Texas at Brownsville and Texas Southmost College, and is the first Mexican-American woman in the nation selected to lead a college or a university. She is widely known for her pioneering effort to design and establish a unique partnership between the pre-existing community college and the newly created University of Texas at Brownsville. Under her leadership the newly created "community university" has grown from 7,300 to almost 14,000 students, expanded its degree offerings to multiple new associate, bachelor's and graduate programs, and transformed a 47-acre community college campus into a 380-acre university campus with new state-of-the-art facilities. In addition, hundreds of well-credentialed faculty members have been recruited to launch new programs in disciplines ranging from physics to environmental sciences, and the quality of the graduates has also been improved dramatically. Research programs in physics and biomedicine have benefited from collaborative efforts with other universities. Dr. Garcia serves on the board of directors for the Public Welfare Foundation, the Ford Foundation, Campus Compact, and the National Audubon Society. She is the former Chair of the American Council on Education and the Advisory Committee to Congress on Student Financial Assistance and the former Vice Chair of the Carnegie Foundation for the Advancement of Teaching. She holds a doctorate in communication and linguistics from The University of Texas at Austin and honorary doctorate degrees from Notre Dame and Brown University.

ERROLL B. DAVIS, JR. serves as Chancellor of the University System of Georgia, a post he took on February 6, 2006. Prior to joining the University System, he served as Chairman of the Board of Alliant Energy Corporation, an energy holding company based in Madison, Wisconsin, with $8.3 billion in total assets and annual operating revenues of $3.0 billion. He holds an MBA in finance from the University of Chicago. He joined Alliant in 1998 as president and chief executive officer. Prior to the creation of Alliant Energy, Davis served as president and CEO of WPL Holdings (Wisconsin Power and Light), from 1990 to 1998. From 1978 to 1990, Erroll rose through the senior management ranks at Wisconsin Power and Light Company, starting as vice president of finance and ending as CEO and president. His career also includes corporate finance positions at Xerox Corporation and Ford Motor Company. Erroll Davis is someone who has a passion about education and has devoted a considerable amount of his personal time and financial resources to this end. He and his wife Elaine established the Davis Family Foundation, which makes annual grants to numerous students in need. He previously served as a member of the University of Wisconsin System Board of Regents, from 1987 to 1994, and as a former Chairman of the Board of Trustees of Carnegie Mellon University, of which he is a life member. He presently serves as a member of the Board of Trustees of the University of Chicago. He also is a member of the Board of Directors of BP p.l.c., PPG Industries, Inc., and Union Pacific Corp., and numerous professional associations and civic organizations. In 2004, he was elected to the U.S. Olympic Committee Board, and chairs the USOC's Audit Committee.

DARYUSH ILA, Alabama A&M University Research Institute, is an expert in ion–matter interactions and has authored or coauthored over 200 publications, five books, and one book chapter in this area. He holds a Ph.D. in condensed matter physics from the University of Massachusetts. At Alabama A&M, an HBCU, he has built up a research program that has garnered over $45 million and has led to the creation of the AAMU Research Institute, a university-owned 501(c)(3) that Dr. Ila founded and directs. He also founded the Center for Irradiation of Materials at AAMU. In addition to his AAMU responsibilities, Dr. Ila is the campus director of the AAMU-Space Grant Consortium (since 1989), Secretary of the South Eastern Section of University Space Research Association (USRA), Director of the Advanced Propulsion Materials Center at AAMU, and Director of the Alabama DoD EPSCoR Program. Dr. Ila has chaired multiple committees in national professional societies. He is a graduate of the Massachusetts Institute of Technology and the University of Massachusetts at Lowell.

WAYNE JOHNSON is the Vice President for Hewlett-Packard Company's University Relations Worldwide, located at HP Laboratories in Palo Alto, California. He is responsible for higher education programs in research, marketing and sales, recruitment, continuing education, public affairs, and philanthropy. Johnson joined HP in July 2001 from Microsoft's University Relations Department, where he managed program managers and administrative staff across a customer base of 50 tier-one universities. From 1967 to 2000, he held a variety of positions at the Raytheon Company in Lexington, Massachusetts, including national sales manager for Wireless Solutions, manager of International Financing and Business Development, manager of Administration and Strategic Planning for Raytheon's Research Division, and manager of Program Development and Operations for Technical Services. Johnson received his B.A. in 1967 from Colgate University, Hamilton, NY and his MBA in 1971 from Boston College's Carroll School, Boston, MA. He serves on the boards of the Anita Borg Institute for Women and Technology (ABIWT), MentorNet (MN), and the Alliance for Science and Technology Research in America (ASTRA). He also belongs to NASA's Educational Advisory Committee, the NSF Corporate Foundation Alliance (CFA), Accreditation Board for Engineering and Technology (ABET) Industrial Advisory Board, and the International Conference on Engineering Education (ICEE), and is a member of the Glion Colloquium, as well as being a member of the President's Council of Olin College. Johnson sponsors and leads the Bay Area Science and Innovation Consortium (BASIC).

VIJAYA MELNICK is Professor Emeritus of Biological and Environmental Sciences and Director of the Office of Sponsored Research & Programs, University of the District of Columbia. She served as the Director of the Center for Applied Research and Urban Policy for a number of years. She is Associate Director, International Center for Interdisciplinary Studies in Immunology, at the Georgetown University Medical Center and a member of the Health Care Ethics Faculty at the Howard University Medical College. She is the First Vice President of the International Health Awareness Network. She has served as a senior science advisor to the Lemelson Center for Inventions & Innovations, National Museum of American History of the Smithsonian Institution; and as a science advisor and member of the faculty of the Einstein Institute for Science Health & the Courts. She has served as principal investigator on several research projects and has authored numerous articles and books. She serves on boards and executive committees of national and international organizations concerned with health and/or education. She received her Ph.D. and postdoctoral training from the University of Wisconsin-Madison.

TERRENCE MILLAR is a professor of mathematics at the University of Wisconsin-Madison, where he has been a faculty member since 1976. He holds a Ph.D. from Cornell University in mathematical logic. At UW, he has held a number of administrative posts, including Acting Associate Vice Chancellor, Interim Director of the Graduate Student Professional Development Office, and currently, Graduate School Associate Dean for the Physical Sciences. He has a strong interest in STEM education, having served as chair of the Wisconsin Mathematics Department's Emerging Scholars Program (the Treisman calculus program intended to improve minority participation and performance), interim co-director of the NSF National Institute for Science Education, chair of an NSF-funded national forum on graduate education, and principal investigator and project director on several NSF-funded STEM grants, including two K-12 grants and (currently) a comprehensive Math-Science Partnership award. He has a strong interest in the meaningful integration of research in the natural sciences, mathematics, and engineering at all levels of education. The subject matter of his publications includes both mathematics (Model Theory and Computable Model Theory) and STEM education (graduate and K-12).

DIANA NATALICIO was named president of the University of Texas at El Paso in 1988. During her long and distinguished career with the university, she has served as Vice President for Academic Affairs, Dean of Liberal Arts, and Chair of the Modern Languages Department. During her tenure as president, UTEP's enrollment has grown to nearly 20,000 students, its annual budget has tripled from $80 million to $250 million, research expenditures have grown from less than $5 million to more than $46 million per year. The number of doctoral programs has increased from one to 14 during this same period. She has served as a member and vice chair of the National Science Board, and her current appointments include the boards of the Rockefeller Foundation, the U.S.-Mexico Foundation for Science, National Action Council for Minorities in Engineering, Trinity Industries, and Sandia Corporation. She is the recipient of the Harold W. McGraw, Jr. Prize in Education, was inducted into the Texas Women's Hall of Fame, and was honored by the Texas Exes with the Distinguished Alumnus Award at The University of Texas at Austin. A graduate of St. Louis University, Dr. Natalicio earned a master's degree in Portuguese and a doctorate in linguistics from the University of Texas at Austin.

T. JOAN ROBINSON is the Provost and Vice President for Academic Affairs at Morgan State University. She received her Ph.D. in endocrinology and cell biology at Howard University in Washington, D.C. After obtaining her degree, she pursued postdoctoral studies at the Mayo Clinic in the laboratory of cellular and molecular biology and at the Laboratory of Chemistry at NIDDK, NIH. Subsequent to this training, she taught and conducted extramurally funded research as an assistant professor at North Carolina A&T State University from 1983 to 1989; as Associate Professor of Pharmacology at Xavier University of Louisiana from 1989 to 1993; as Professor and Chair of the Biology Department at Morgan State University from 1993 to 1998; and as Professor and Dean of the School of Computer, Mathematical and Natural Sciences from 1998 to 2004. Throughout her academic career, Dr. Robinson has trained post-doctoral fellows, several graduate, and undergraduate students in the research laboratory. Dr. Robinson's research career has garnered grant awards totaling approximately $40 million from the National Institutes of Health through programs such as RCMI, RIMI, MARC, BRIDGES, MBRS, and K.14 awards; and from the National Science Foundation. Dr. Robinson has also received the Outstanding Chairperson Award and the Outstanding Award in Grantsmanship at Morgan State University, the Most Distinguished Ph.D. Alumnus at Howard University, and the Minority Access 2001 National Role Model Award. She was also named Woman of the Year for 2003 by the American Bibliographic Institute. Currenty, Dr. Robinson serves as a member of the National Advisory General Medical Sciences Council and on the University Board of Trustees, Carlow University, Pittsburgh, PA. In the past, she served as a consultant to and as Chair of the National Institute of General Medical Science (NIGMS)/Minority Biomedical Research Support (MBRS) Subcommittee Review Panel; as President of the Program Directors' Organization for the Research Infrastructure in Minority Institution (RIMI) Program, and as a consultant on the U.S. Army Science Board where she provided advice to the Secretary of the Army on science and related matters. Dr. Robinson is also the co-editor of the *International Journal of Cellular and Molecular Biology*.

JUAN M. SANCHEZ is the Vice President for Research at the University of Texas at Austin and holder of the Temple Foundation Endowed Professorship #4 in the Department of Mechanical Engineering. He obtained his B.S. in Physics at the University of Cordoba, Argentina, and completed his M.S. and Ph.D. in Materials Science at the University of California, Los Angeles. Dr. Sanchez is the author and co-author of over 140 technical publications on a wide range of topics in materials science and engineering. His current research interests are in the electronic, thermodynamic and structural properties of materials including intermetallic compounds, magnetic and non-magnetic alloys, thin films and magnetic multilayers. Dr. Sanchez serves on the Council of Federal Relations of the Association of American Universities and on the Board of Directors as Council Vice

Chair for the Oak Ridge Associated Universities and the Texas Nanotechnology Initiative. He also serves as a Representative to the Government-University-Industry Research Roundtable of the National Academies, as Trustee for the Southeastern Universities Research Association, Inc., as a Board Member of the Institutional Oversight Committee for the National Partnership for Advanced Computing Infrastructure (NPACI), the Board of Visitors of the US Army War College, Member of the International Consulting Board, Advisory Board for the Texas Coalition for Capital, the National Scientific and Policy Advisory Council for the Hogg Foundation for Mental Health, and member of the AusTech Alliance of the Greater Austin Chamber of Commerce.

MARCUS SHUTE currently serves as Vice President for Research and Sponsored Programs and Professor in the College of Engineering, Technology, and Computer Science at Tennessee State University, an HBCU. During his career, Dr. Shute has served as a project team leader and Distinguished Member of Technical Staff at Bell Laboratories, AT&T and Lucent Technologies; as Vice President of Engineering and as Vice President of Advanced Technologies at Luxcore Networks, Inc., an optical networking systems start-up company; CEO of Shute Enterprises, Inc., a consulting firm; President and Chairman of Nile Valle Investment Group, Inc., a real estate investment company; and co-founder and director of Aspire 2B, Inc. He has a Ph.D. in mechanical engineering from the Georgia Institute of Technology and has published extensively and acquired patents in the areas of optical fiber communications, wireless communications, optical fiber amplifiers, planar waveguide technology, polarization phenomena, and electronic materials.

Appendix B

Workshop Agenda

Partnerships for Emerging Research Institutions
September 13, 2007
The National Academies
Keck Building
Room 100
500 Fifth St. NW, Washington, DC

8:00 – 8:20 am Welcome, History, and Background of the Workshop

- **Dr. Juliet V. Garcia**, Chair, Committee on Partnerships for Emerging Research Institutions; President, the University of Texas at Brownsville and Texas Southmost College (20 min)

8:20 – 8:50 am Why We Do Research—Perspectives of Smaller Institutions

(Moderator: T. Joan Robinson, Provost and Vice President for Academic Affairs, Morgan State University)

- The Merit of Undergraduate Research: A Confluence of Student, Faculty, and Institutional Rewards
    - **Dr. Kerry Karukstis**, President, Council for Undergraduate Research, Professor of Chemistry, Harvey Mudd College (15 min)
- Research: A Necessary Component of Education
    - **Dr. Eugene Collins**, Natural Sciences and Mathematics Division Director, Fisk University (15 min)

8:50 – 9:00 am Audience Q&A

9:00 – 9:30 am How does teaching and administrative support at Emerging Research Institutions impact faculty's ability to conduct research? – A Faculty Panel Overview
(Moderator: Juan Sanchez, Vice President for Research, University of Texas at Austin)

- **Dr. Terrance Johnson,** Chair, Department of Biological Sciences, Tennessee State University (10 min)
- **Dr. Mario Díaz**, Professor of Physics and Director, Center for Gravitational Wave Astronomy, The University of Texas at Brownsville (10 min)
- **Dr. Arlene Cole-Rhodes**, Associate Professor, Department of Electrical & Computer Engineering, Morgan State University (10 min)

9:30 – 10:00 am Faculty Panel Discussion with Audience

10:00 – 10:15 am BREAK

10:15 – 11:15 am "If I'm Teaching 7 Courses a Semester, How Can I Find Time for Research?"
(Moderator: Erroll Davis, Chancellor, University System of Georgia)

- Aligning Reward Systems to Institutional Missions: Balancing Access and Excellence
  - **Dr. Benjamin Flores**, Associate Dean of Engineering Graduate Studies and Research, Department of Electrical and Computer Engineering, University of Texas at El Paso (15 min)
- Making a Full Plate Less Full: Finding Time for Research
  - **Dr. Dorothy Zinsmeister**, Assistant Vice Chancellor for Academic Affairs, University System of Georgia (15 min)
- Dedicated Semester for Research: State-Funded Faculty Development Program
  - **Dr. Jim Muyskens**, President, Queens College, Former Senior Vice Chancellor for Academic Affairs for the University System of Georgia (15 min)

- o **Dr. Alan Gabrielli,** Dean, School of Arts and Sciences, Southern Polytechnic State University (7 min)
- o **Dr. Kent Barefield**, Associate Dean, College of Sciences, Georgia Institute of Technology (7 min)

11:15 – 11:25 am Audience Q&A

11:25 – 12:15 pm WORKING LUNCH – Topical Tables

(Moderator: Terrence Millar, Professor of Mathematics; Associate Dean for the Physical Sciences, Graduate School, University of Wisconsin-Madison)

- Faculty Reward/Incentive Systems for Conducting Research
- Making Efficient Use of Faculty Teaching Time
- Pre-Award/Post Award Administrative Support
- Tech Transfer Support
- State-Wide Journal Subscription Sharing
- Administrative Mentoring Programs

12:15 – 1:15 pm Successful Experiments in "Partnerships for Administrative Capacity-Building" Part I

(Moderator: Daryush Ila, Professor of Physics and Executive Director, Alabama A&M University Research Institute)

- Army Small Business Program
  - o **Tracey Pinson**, Director, Office of Small Business Programs, Department of the Army (20 min)
- Supporting & Developing the Capacity of Two Native Communities to Conduct Research (joint presentation, 20 min)
  - o **Susan Ross**, Director, Evanston Unit, Northwestern University
  - o **Adam Kessel**, Education Developer, American Indian Center of Chicago
- Simplifying Grant Administration (20 min)
  - o **Janet Polli**, Associate, Research Foundation of CUNY

1:15 – 1:25 pm Audience Q&A

1:25 – 1:40 pm BREAK

1:40 – 2:40 pm Successful Experiments in "Partnerships for Administrative Capacity-Building" Part II
(Moderator: Marcus Shute, Vice President for Research and Sponsored Programs and Professor in the College of Engineering, Technology, and Computer Science, Tennessee State University)

- Acquiring Tech Transfer Expertise
  - Challenges of Research Administration at a Small Institution
    Karen Mitchell, Director, Office of Sponsored Projects and Research, University of the Sciences in Philadelphia (20 min)
  - Maximizing the Value of Federal Research at Emerging Research Institutions
    Tanaga Boozer, President, Intellectual Property Solutions, Inc. (20 min)
- Creating Intellectual Capacity Through Collaboration: GALILEO, Virtual Libraries, and Consortia
  - **Merryll Penson**, Executive Director, Library Services, University System of Georgia (20 min)

2:40 – 2:50 pm Audience Q&A

2:50 – 3:30 pm Town Hall: Barriers and Practical Obstacles to Capacity-Building
(Moderator: Juliet V. Garcia, Committee Chair, Partnerships for ERIs; President, the University of Texas at Brownsville and Texas Southmost College)

3:30 – 4:55 pm From the Research Funding Agencies: Initiatives, Opportunities and Perspectives on Building the Capacity to do Research
(Moderator: Vijaya Melnick, Professor Emeritus of Biological and Environmental Sciences and Director of the Office of Sponsored Research and Programs, University of the District of Columbia)

- Help Is on the Way: The Federal Demonstration Partnership and Emerging Research Institutions
  - **David Wright**, Executive Director, Federal Demonstration Partnership (15 min)
- The NIH Extramural Associates Program: Enhancing Research Capacity in Women & Minority-Serving Institutions in the U.S. and Developing Countries
  - **Dr. Regina James**, Director, Extramural Associates Program, National Institute of Child Health and Human Development (NICHD), NIH (15 min)
- National Science Foundation - Funding Opportunities and Resources
  - **Dr. Denise Barnes**, Program Director, National Science Foundation, Experimental Program to Stimulate Competitive Research (15 min)

Audience Q&A

4:55 – 5:00 pm **Dr. Juliet V. Garcia**, Chair, Committee on Partnerships for Emerging Research Institutions; President, the University of Texas at Brownsville and Texas Southmost College (5 min)

5:00 – 6:00 pm Reception

September 14, 2007

The National Academies

Keck Building

Room 105

500 Fifth St. NW, Washington, DC

8:00 a.m. – 12:00 p.m.

Attendance is limited to 20

Roadmapping Workshop for Senior Academic Officers of Emerging Research Institutions

This roadmapping session will be limited to a small group—first come, first served—of senior academic officers from Emerging Research Institutions interested in developing an action plan for increasing their own institution's level of research activity. On hand will be representatives from institutions that have recently surmounted the $100K/faculty member research funding threshold, to discuss in a step-by-step manner specific activities that can be used to progressively increase institutional capacity. This session will be professionally facilitated so that each person leaves with an action plan tailored to his/her institution.

Appendix C

Workshop Participants

Theresa Bailey
The University of Texas-Pan American

Megan Bang
American Indian Center of Chicago

Kent Barefield
Georgia Institute of Technology

Denise Barnes
National Science Foundation

Richard Bissell
The National Academies

Henry Blount
National Science Foundation

Dawn Boatman
University of North Florida

Robert Bolla
Bradley University

Tanaga Boozer
Intellectual Property Solutions

Arlene Cole-Rhodes
Morgan State University

W. Eugene Collins
Fisk University

Janice Cuny
National Science Foundation

Erroll B. Davis, Jr.
Board of Regents of the University System of Georgia

Mario Diaz
University of Texas at Brownsville

Catherine Didion
National Academy of Engineering

Imeh Ebong
University of North Florida

Denise Ehlen
University of Wisconsin-Whitewater

Benjamin Flores
University of Texas at El Paso

Cathy Fore
Oak Ridge Associated Universities

Alan Gabrielli
Southern Polytechnic State University

Juliet Garcia
University of Texas at Brownsville

Robert Gracy
University of Texas at San Antonio

Denise Greene
The National Academies

Robert Hampton
Tennessee State University

Nancy Hensel
Council on Undergraduate Research

Daryush Ila
Alabama A&M University Research Institute

Regina James
National Institutes of Health

Terrance Johnson
Tennessee State University

Mary Juhas
National Science Foundation

Kerry Karukstis
Harvey Mudd College

Adam Kessel
Northwestern University

Charlotte Kuh
The National Academies

Bruce Landman
University of West Georgia

Edward Lee
Air Force Office of Scientific Research

Arlene Maclin
Norfolk State University

Chris Maples
Desert Research Institute

José Martín
The University of Texas at Brownsville

Merrilea Mayo
The National Academies

Jeffrey McKinnon
University of Wisconsin-Whitewater

Vijaya Melnick
University of the District of Columbia

Terry Millar
University of Wisconsin-Madison

Karen Mitchell
University of the Sciences in Philadelphia

James Muyskens
Queens College, City University of New York

John Nemeth
Oak Ridge Associated Universities

Mildred Ofosu
Morgan State University

Camellia Okpodu
Norfolk State University

Merryll Penson
Board of Regents of the University System of Georgia

Tracey Pinson
Department of Army, Office of Small Business Programs

Janet Polli
Research Foundation of The City University of New York

Earnestine Psalmonds
The National Academies

Wilhelmina Reuben-Cooke
University of the District of Columbia

T. Joan Robinson
Morgan State University

Susan Ross
Northwestern University

Juan M. Sanchez
University of Texas at Austin

Marcus W. Shute
Tennessee State University

Mary Stephens-Frazier
Morgan State University

Susan Su
National Academy of Engineering

Maria Thompson
Tennessee State Univesity

James Till
California State University, Long Beach

David Travis
University of Wisconsin-Whitewater

Gerald Van Hecke
Harvey Mudd College

Jodi Wesemann
American Chemical Society

Kevin Whittlesey
Office of Representative Doris Matsui

David Wright
Federal Demonstration Partnership

Dorothy Zinsmeister
Board of Regents of the University System of Georgia

Cindy Zook
Cindy Zook Associates

Appendix D

2005 Basic Carnegie Classification: Distribution of Institutions and Enrollments

Category	
Assoc/Pub-R-S: Associate's—Public Rural-serving, Small	
Assoc/Pub-R-M: Associate's—Public Rural-serving, Medium	
Assoc/Pub-R-L: Associate's—Public Rural-serving, Large	
Assoc/Pub-S-SC: Associate's—Public Suburban-serving, Single Campus	
Assoc/Pub-S-MC: Associate's—Public Suburban-serving, Multicampus	
Assoc/Pub-U-SC: Associate's—Public Urban-serving, Single Campus	
Assoc/Pub-U-MC: Associate's—Public Urban-serving, Multicampus	
Assoc/Pub-Spec: Associate's—Public special use	
Assoc/PrivNFP: Associate's—Private not-for-profit	
Assoc/PrivFP4: Associate's—Private for-profit	
Assoc/Pub2in4: Associate's—Public 2-year colleges under 4-year universities	
Assoc/Pub4: Associate's—Public 4-year Primarily Associate's	
Assoc/PrivNFP4: Associate's—Private not-for-profit 4-year Primarily Associate's	
Assoc/PrivFP4: Associate's—Private for-profit 4-year Primarily Associate's	
RU/VH: Research Universities (very high research activity)	
RU/H: Research Universities (high research activity)	
DRU: Doctoral/Research Universities	
Master's L: Master's Colleges and Universities (larger programs)	
Master's M: Master's Colleges and Universities (medium programs)	
Master's S: Master's Colleges and Universities (smaller programs)	**ERIs**
Bac/A&S: Baccalaureate Colleges—Arts & sciences	
Bac/Diverse: Baccalaureate Colleges—Diverse fields	
Bac/Assoc: Baccalaureate/Associate's Colleges	
Spec/Faith: Special Focus Institutions—Theological seminaries, Bible colleges, and other faith-related institutions	
Spec/Med: Special Focus Institutions—Medical schools and medical centers	
Spec/Health: Special Focus Institutions—Other health professions schools	
Spec/Engg: Special Focus Institutions—Schools of engineering	
Spec/Tech: Special Focus Institutions—Other technology-related schools	
Spec/Bus: Special Focus Institutions—Schools of business and management	
Spec/Arts: Special Focus Institutions—Schools of art, music, and design	
Spec/Law: Special Focus Institutions—Schools of law	
Spec/Other: Special Focus Institutions—Other special-focus institutions	
Tribal: Tribal Colleges	**ERIs**
(Not classified)	
All Institutions	

NOTE: (1) Branch campuses are counted separately if reported separately in IPEDS.
(2) Fall enrollment may not reflect the total number of students served over the course of a year.
(3) Percentage details may not sum to 100 due to rounding.
SOURCES: 2005 Carnegie Classification; National Center for Education Statistics, IPEDS Fall Enrollment (2004).

Institutions	Percent	Total Enrollment	Percent
142	3.20%	133,027	0.80%
311	7.10%	943,701	5.40%
144	3.30%	1,087,790	6.20%
110	2.50%	854,259	4.90%
100	2.30%	1,051,012	6.00%
32	0.70%	275,307	1.60%
152	3.50%	1,743,179	9.90%
14	0.30%	30,220	0.20%
114	2.60%	43,961	0.30%
532	12.10%	273,368	1.60%
55	1.30%	134,222	0.80%
18	0.40%	148,416	0.80%
20	0.50%	12,052	0.10%
71	1.60%	48,272	0.30%
96	2.20%	2,365,228	13.50%
103	2.30%	1,693,731	9.60%
83	1.90%	848,316	4.80%
347	7.90%	2,815,954	16.00%
190	4.30%	739,648	4.20%
128	2.90%	349,859	2.00%
286	6.50%	524,229	3.00%
360	8.20%	595,754	3.40%
120	2.70%	267,832	1.50%
314	7.10%	101,742	0.60%
57	1.30%	90,701	0.50%
129	2.90%	59,634	0.30%
8	0.20%	14,259	0.10%
57	1.30%	40,160	0.20%
64	1.50%	92,222	0.50%
106	2.40%	128,273	0.70%
32	0.70%	25,683	0.10%
39	0.90%	17,796	0.10%
32	0.70%	17,599	0.10%
26	0.60%	3,698	0.00%
4,392	100.00%	17,571,104	100.00%

Appendix E

Roadmap for Emerging Research Institutions

Goal	Key Results	Key Strategies	12-Month Action Plan
Create a compelling/value-added niche for research	Clearly identified and articulated areas of strength Flow of external funding into areas of expertise Presence of niche in University marketing materials	Develop searchable research capabilities database Create college strategic plans outlining areas of strength Identify partners who align with and complement strengths	Inventory existing capabilities Identify potential customers and partners for joint ventures Create strategy to fill expertise gaps Survey the market opportunities
Cultivate top-level champions or advocates	Research articulated as a top goal for the university by the president; president speaks publicly about research and invests accordingly Fundraising by president targeted for research Allocation of x% of university resources to research Senior administration and faculty governance advocates for research and research productivity measures in assessment, promotion, evaluation, and salary decisions	Frame the research program in terms that align with the university mission Sponsor informal dialogues on ways to help faculty to engage in research Develop a compelling business case Present the results of other ERI benchmarks Involve president, research administrator, and local business people in jointly defining a strategy Map existing relationships	Use capabilities inventory as seeds of a vision and business case Convene forum to build shared vision and strategy

Engage faculty and students fully in research projects.	Core of active researchers Increased proposal submissions and grant awards Doubling of publications with student co-authors Well-established research centers attracting faculty and students	Identify critical mass of faculty by interest and capabilities Publicize incentives for research Create faculty learning communities for research collaboration	Create and market the incentive plan and get endorsement Allocate research incentive funds Identify and pursue large grant opportunities
Engage external stakeholders	Regional and national visibility and recognition $x appropriated state and federal funds $x targeted donations from industry and local organizations	"Big events" around successes Effective networks of stakeholders Research advisory group Articulated value to the regional market	Develop a stakeholder map of interests and goals Get stakeholders' feedback to research vision
Develop a robust infrastructure for research business operations	A proactive, strategic, responsive, knowledgeable CP for business affairs Streamlined business systems – efficiency and effectiveness	Graphically map key business processes Develop and track performance and customer satisfaction metrics Inventory research facilities and align with the needs of research centers Educate administrators about the importance of their roles in supporting research Develop cross-divisional working groups to streamline business processes	Revised flow chart with streamlined system Engage all constituents to plan implementation of changes

continued

Goal	Key Results	Key Strategies	12-Month Action Plan
Establish an office of intellectual property	Professional staff and patent counsel Effective intellectual property policies and committee Intellectual property disclosures and licensed technologies	Examine best practices Hire an experienced professional Educate the campus regarding IP policies and procedures Visibly reward faculty efforts	Identify prospects for IP disclosure Develop benchmarks (refer to AUTM) Allocate funds to support the position, operations, and IP portfolio Market IP assets to companies